OUTDOOR LIFE

essential

FISHING

for teens

Ron Fitzgerald

HIGH
interest
books

Children's Press
A Division of Grolier Publishing
New York / London / Hong Kong / Sydney
Danbury, Connecticut

Contributing Editors: Jennifer Ceaser and Rob Kirkpatrick
Book Design: Nelson Sa
Photo Credits: Cover, pp. 5, 6, 9, 10, 12, © Index Stock Photography, Inc.; pp. 13, 14, 15, 16, 18, 20 © Haley Wilson; pp. 22, 25 © Index Stock Photography, Inc.; pp. 26, 29 © Image Bank; pp. 30, 32 © Index Stock Photography, Inc.; pp. 35, 41 © Allsport

Library of Congress Cataloging-in-Publication Data

Fitzgerald, Ron.
    Essential fishing for teens / by Ron Fitzgerald.
        p. cm. – (Outdoor life)
    Includes bibliographical references and index.
    Summary: Presents information about fishing, including an explanation of the different types of fishing, the equipment needed, and safety tips.
    ISBN 0-516-23355-6 (lib. bdg.) – ISBN 0-516-23555-9 (pbk.)
        1. Fishing—Juvenile literature. [1. Fishing.] I Title. II. Outdoor life (Children's Press)

    SH445.F58 2000
    799.1—dc21

                                                           00-023359

CONTENTS

INTRODUCTION

So you want to catch a fish. It certainly sounds easy enough. First you find some water, then you catch a fish. Yet fishing isn't as easy as it might seem at first. There are many kinds of fish and many different ways to catch them. You need the right equipment and you need to learn how to use it. You need to know the rules and regulations for fishing in a particular area. Safety also is an essential part of fishing.

Once you've learned all of these aspects of fishing, then you will be able to enjoy the sport. Fishing, also called angling, is fun, challenging, and a great way to enjoy nature. This book will help you become familiar with fishing and will give you tips on how to be a good angler.

Fishing is a fun and challenging sport.

1
TYPES OF FISHING

Fishing can be done in freshwater areas,
such as a river or stream.

Wherever there is water, there are almost always fish. The type of fish will depend on the type of water. There are two kinds of water: freshwater and saltwater. Saltwater, such as the ocean, has salt in it. Freshwater, such as a river, does not. Here are the most common types of fishing and the kinds of fish you will be likely to catch in freshwater and saltwater.

BAIT FISHING

Bait fishing, also called still fishing, is the oldest and most common type of fishing. It involves very basic equipment: a rod, a reel, a hook, and bait. Usually, bait fishing is done in freshwater areas such as rivers, lakes, and creeks. The angler stands near or wades into the water. Then he or she casts (throws) a fishing line into the water. When bait fishing, you can expect to catch bass, catfish, crappies, and perch.

BOAT FISHING

There are times when a boat is needed to get you to where the fish are. There are almost as many kinds of boats as there are types of fish. They include rowboats, motorboats, sailboats, and canoes.

One type of boat fishing is trolling. A baited fishing line is pulled slowly through the water by a motor-powered boat. Trolling can be done in both freshwater and saltwater. Trout, pike, tuna, and salmon are the types of fish usually caught when trolling.

FLY-FISHING

Fly-fishing is different from other types of fishing because you are constantly casting your rod. (With other types of fishing, you cast and wait for the fish to bite.) Because so much casting is involved, a very light rod must be used.

Sailboats are one type of boat used to get you to where the fish are.

At one time, fly anglers used live flies as bait. Today, most of them use artificial (fake) flies. Trout, pike, and salmon are popular catches when fly-fishing.

BIG-GAME FISHING

Big-game fishing gets its name from the size of the fish after which you are going. Big-game fishing means big fish and big water. If you plan to go after these monsters of the deep, you will need to go out into the ocean on a large, motor-powered fishing boat. These boats are equipped with seats that are attached to the boat. Huge metal fishing rods are mounted to the chairs. Marlin, swordfish, tuna, and even sharks are caught by big-game anglers.

Big-game fishing boats have chairs attached to the deck or sides of the boat.

2
Fishing Equipment

Fishing equipment includes a rod and reel.

Fishing basically involves a rod, a reel, and some bait. You can catch a fish with a stick, a piece of string, and a worm. But if you want to get serious, you will need the right tools. Different methods of fishing call for different equipment. Fishing equipment—from rod and reel to hook, line, and sinker—is called tackle.

HOOK

A hook usually is made of steel. It is curved with a barb (sharp point) at the end. Hooks may have more than one barb. They come in many sizes and shapes. Remember, the hook has to fit in the mouth of the fish. Be sure to get the right size hook for the type of fish you want to catch.

Hook sizes for catching the average fish are based on a numbering system. The hooks are numbered from the smallest (#20) to the largest (#0). Anything larger than #0 is used to catch big-game fish. Large hooks also are numbered from the smallest (#1/0) to the largest (#20/0).

LINE

The fishing line is what brings the bait out to the fish. It also brings the fish in to you. The line runs from the reel, along the rod, and out to the hook.

There are many kinds of fishing line. In small lakes and rivers, most anglers use an 8- to 15-pound test line. This means that the line can support a fish that weighs 15 pounds (6.5 kg) or less. For fishing in the ocean, anglers might use a 50- to 100-pound-plus test line. The line you use depends on which type of fish you are trying to catch. A big fish will break a thin line. A small fish will notice a bigger line and might be scared away.

LEADER

A leader is a short piece of line that connects the hook to the main fishing line. Usually, the leader is a bit thinner than the rest of the fishing line. That way, the fish will not see the line when it zooms in on the baited hook.

SINKER

A sinker is a small weight. It makes the fishing line and hook sink in the water. A sinker brings the bait down to where the fish are. There are many types of sinkers, but most beginning anglers use small metal balls, called split shot sinkers. These sinkers open and snap back together around the fishing line.

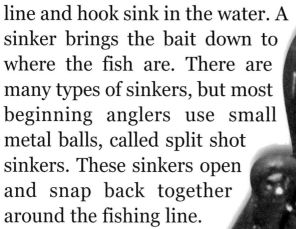

BOBBER

A bobber is a lightweight object made of wood or plastic. It snaps onto the fishing line and floats on top of the water. A bobber helps you to see when you have a bite on your line. The bobber moves when a fish tugs on the line. Of course, the bobber also moves as it floats on the water. With time and experience, you will recognize the way a bobber moves when you have a bite.

BAIT AND LURES

Bait is put on a hook to lure a fish into biting it. Many anglers think natural bait works the best. Natural bait includes worms, cheese, and small fish. Other anglers prefer the ease of using man-made lures. Lures are made to look like the food fish like to eat. There are many different kinds of lures. Some are very small and look like flies. Others are much bigger and look like fish or worms. The following are some of the most common types of lures.

- **Plugs** Plugs look like the little fish that big fish like to eat. Some plugs are made to skim along the top of the water. Others will "swim" beneath the surface like real fish.
- **Jigs** Jigs are made with feathers or plastic "hair" to attract fish. An angler must make the jig dart and zoom like a small fish to get a bigger fish to bite.
- **Spoons and Spinners** These are metal lures that wiggle and flash as they zip through the water. They are made to look like the shiny scales of small fish, such as minnows.
- **Plastic Worms** Tired of losing your worm? Plastic worms look real and can be used again and again.

- **Flies** These lures are made to look like flies and other small bugs.

ROD

Fishing rods come in a lot of different lengths and weights. You should buy a rod based on the type of fishing you will be doing. Longer rods are used to pull big fish out of the ocean. Shorter rods are better for lakes, rivers and streams. Rods can be anywhere from 5 to 15 feet (1.5 to 4.5 m) in length. Beginners may find rods in the 4- to 5-foot (122 to 152 cm) range easiest to handle. Rods range from ultra lightweight—those used to catch 1-pound (.5-kg) fish—to heavy—for 6- to 10-pound (2.5- to 4.5-kg) fish.

All fishing rods have line guides. Line guides are the small metal rings along the rod. The fishing line runs through the line guides from the hook into the reel. Guides help to keep your line tangle-free.

You can find a good freshwater rod for about $25 to $40. Good fly-fishing rods can be found in the $50 to $70 range. Fly-fishing rods are lighter and stronger than are other freshwater rods, so they are more expensive. Saltwater rods usually are larger and sturdier than freshwater rods. They also are more expensive, at around $60 to $90. Saltwater rods need to be strong because of the size of the fish and the strength of the ocean current.

REEL

Along with a rod, you must have a reel. The reel controls your fishing line. The reel lets the line out when you cast. It also brings the line back in again. There are different reels for different types of fishing.

There are three basic types of fishing reels: closed-face reel, spinning reel, and baitcasting reel. Each of these reels is used for a different kind of fishing. Make sure that you buy the correct type of reel for your rod. Also, make sure your reel fits your rod. Good anglers will balance their rod and their reel.

Closed-Face Reel

A closed-face reel is easy to spot because of its cone-shaped cover. It is the easiest type of rod to use and is good for beginning anglers. You cast by pushing a button that releases the line.

Spinning Reel

Fishing with a spinning reel is a bit more difficult than using a closed-face reel. If you want to catch bigger fish—those in the 10- to 12- pound (4.5 to 5.4 kg) range—you will need to have a spinning reel.

A spinning reel has a drag, which can be turned to adjust the amount of pull on the fishing line. Turn the drag counter-clockwise to loosen the tension when a fish pulls on the line. This keeps the line from breaking. If it's a very large fish, you may need to turn off the drag and use just your reel to bring in the fish.

Baitcasting Reel

A baitcasting reel is the most difficult type of reel to cast. However, if you want to catch large fish (anywhere from 12 pounds to hundreds of pounds), you need to know how to use one. A baitcasting reel is made to hold a heavy line, which is necessary to catch large fish.

A common frustration when using a baitcasting reel is backlash. Backlash happens when the spool, which holds the line, spins too quickly as you cast. The spool releases the line faster than the line can go out. The line becomes tangled and may need to be replaced. You will likely need quite a bit of practice before you can cast with this type of reel.

FLY-FISHING EQUIPMENT

Fly-fishing requires its own special equipment. You will need a fly-fishing rod, which usually is 7 to 10 feet (2 to 3 m) in length. The rods are very thin and light. A simple reel is all that is required, as the rod and line are much more important. The line is heavy and is specially designed to taper (narrow) at the end.

Fly-fishers use artificial flies to imitate the three life stages of a fly. A nymph is made to sink to the bottom. It resembles a fly larva (wingless baby). Dry flies are made of a material that floats. A dry fly looks like a healthy, adult fly floating on top of the water. A wet fly is designed to drift underwater. It looks like a drowned fly.

Artificial flies are made of many types of materials and in various colors. You can find flies made out of fur, feathers, thread, tinsel, and wool.

Fly-fishing requires its own special equipment.

Fishing Tip

When using natural bait, the trick is to find a kind that works. Some fish may not go for worms. They may like minnows instead. Watch what the fish are eating. If you can figure out their favorite food, you will catch more fish.

WHERE TO BUY EQUIPMENT

Fishing equipment can be found in most large stores that have a sporting goods department. You also can buy your gear at tackle shops. If there is good fishing in an area, there probably will be a good tackle shop nearby.

Your best bet is to find a tackle shop with good salespeople. They will help you to choose equipment that fits both your fishing needs and your budget. They also may know of great places to fish.

One place you can purchase fishing equipment is in a tackle shop.

3
CASTING

You'll need to learn how to cast before you can hook a fish.

Now you have the tools of an angler. You have the correct size rod and reel. You have fishing line, sinkers, and hooks. You just need to know how to use them.

CASTING

Casting is throwing your line into the water. Your casting method will depend on the fishing equipment you are using. With a closed-face reel or a spinning reel, use the following technique:

- **Hold the rod in your throwing hand.** Point the tip of the rod to about ten o'clock (if you're right-handed) or two o'clock (if you're left-handed). Pull about 6 inches (15 cm) of line off the tip. Reel in any extra line by turning the reel handle in a clockwise motion. Keep your elbow close to your body. You will not

Fishing Tip

When casting, don't try to throw the line into the water. A nice easy snap of the rod will get your line out to the fish.

need to move your arm much. The rod will do most of the work.

- **Bring the tip of the rod back and over your head.**
This move should be nice and smooth. Bring the rod back by bending your elbow. You do not need to move your entire arm. (The rod is long enough to keep the hook away from your head.) The top of the rod should be above your head, as your hand passes by your ear. Keep the rod pointed slightly behind you.

- **Snap the rod forward.**
This motion should feel as though you are flicking paint off a paintbrush. The idea is to snap your wrist forward and let the line fly away from you. Use your arm

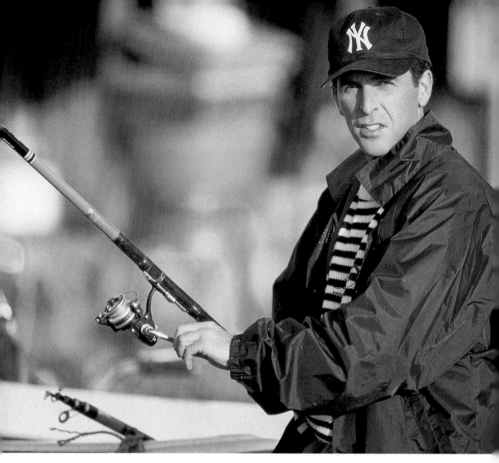

After you've cast, your rod should be out in front of your body, in the spot at which you were aiming.

and wrist to snap the rod forward. This motion will cause the line to zip away from you. Let your arm continue down slowly. You should finish with the tip of your rod pointing at the spot at which you were aiming.

If you are using a closed-face reel, you will need to release the line manually. When the rod is in the starting position over your head, push in the button. Follow the same motion as above, but as you near the ten o'clock (or two o'clock) position, release the line. (The line should zip away from you.)

When practicing with a baitcasting reel, you will want to follow the same steps as above except when you actually cast. The forward motion should be a slow lob, rather than a quick flick. As the line goes out, you will need to put light pressure on the spool using your thumb. These actions will prevent backlash.

Casting with a fly-fishing rod is known as backcasting. As with normal casting, start with the rod in front of you. Bring it behind you. Then, instead of snapping the rod forward with your forearm, flick it forward using your wrist. It should feel as though you are cracking a whip.

Fly-fishing requires a special cast that should feel as though you are cracking a whip.

4
Let's Fish!

An important part of fishing is learning techniques
from a more experienced angler.

Now that you've perfected your cast, you need to choose a place to fish. Earth is two-thirds water. That means that there are plenty of spots in which to fish. There are oceans, lakes, rivers, ponds, and creeks, to name a few. But how do you find a good spot? There are some general things to keep in mind when looking for an area to fish.

- Fish like to eat. They will hang out in places where there is food.
- Fish are easily frightened. They need somewhere to hide from predators. Their hiding place is often where there are weeds or rocks.
- Fish are lazy. Swimming in rough water is hard work. So, fish often will rest in the calm water behind rocks and other large objects.

RIGGING AND BAITING

You've got the equipment, you've practiced your cast, and you've found the perfect fishing spot. Just a few more preparations, and you'll be ready to fish!

When you put together your line, it is called rigging. Rigging involves attaching a hook, sinker, and, depending on where you are fishing, a bobber. You also need to put the lure or bait on the hook.

First, tie the hook onto the end of the line. Remember that the hook is extremely sharp, so be very careful not to injure yourself. Next, put a split shot on the line about 6 inches (15 cm) from the hook. Snap on a bobber about 2 feet (60 cm) from the split shot. Now you are ready to bait the hook.

Fish can be picky eaters. Choosing the right bait or lure is very important. It should be presented to the fish as naturally as possible. Try to hide the hook when you use live bait. A fish

Be sure that your line is properly rigged before you start fishing.

will not bite something that looks strange. Do not use a gigantic hook for small bait or lures. Do not use heavy sinkers that pull the bait along the bottom. The idea is to make the bait look as though it is floating or swimming in the water.

START FISHING!

Cast your line into the water and wait for the fish to start biting. You may want to give your rod a little jerk now and again to get the fish interested. Watch your bobber closely. If it starts bobbing up and down, it means that a fish is nibbling. Give a quick tug to catch the hook in the fish's mouth. Don't yank too hard or you will tear the bait from its mouth.

If you tug and something tugs back, you've got a fish! Now begin to reel it in slowly. If your reel has a drag, you will need to adjust it. If the fish is pulling out line faster than you can reel it in, you need to tighten the drag. If the line is stretching and your rod is bending, loosen the drag or your line will break. With a combination of adjusting the drag and reeling, you will be able to bring in the fish.

CATCH AND RELEASE

Once you've reeled in your fish, you can do one of two things. You can keep the fish (if the law allows it) or you can throw it back. Most fishing organizations encourage anglers to catch and release whenever possible. You must release the fish if it is under the weight limit set by your state's Fish and Game Commission. You also must release the fish if it is a protected species.

Simply letting the fish go after capturing it is not all there is to catch-and-release fishing. If the fish is released in poor condition, it is likely to die anyway. Here are some guidelines for catch-and-release fishing:

- When you have hooked a fish, try to reel it in as soon as possible. A long battle with a fish can be exciting. However, the most likely outcome for a struggling fish is that it will die.
- Most hooks have barbs on the ends. However, some hooks are made without barbs and are easier to remove from the fish. Barbless hooks also are less harmful to the fish. You can make your own

Fishing Tip

Fishing laws are different from state to state. Your state's Fish and Game Commission sets aside specific times of the year during which you can fish (fishing seasons). Be sure to check with the office in your area for information about fishing licenses, seasons, and limits.

barbless hooks by crushing the barbs flat with a pair of pliers.

- If you must remove the fish from the water, do so as gently as possible. Try not to hang a large fish on the line by its lower jaw or gills. This places a lot of strain on the fish's throat and can cause fatal injuries. Instead, place your hand flat underneath the fish and lift it gently out of the water by its side.

- Have a good place to put the fish while you work on removing the hook. Lay down a wet towel or a damp cloth on the area. Always wet your hands before handling the fish so that you do not tear off its scales.

- If the fish's lip is hooked with a barbless hook, removing the hook will be simple. Let the water support the fish, grab the hook (with a pair of pliers if necessary), and then turn the hook back to release the fish.
- If the hook is in the fish's mouth, gills, throat, or somewhere you can see it, you usually can remove the hook using a pair of pliers. If you can see the hook, but you cannot get it out, try to cut the hook where it bends. This will help the fish get rid of the hook by itself.
- If the fish already has swallowed the bait, try to cut off the line as close to its mouth as possible. Then let the fish swim away. The fish usually will be able to get rid of the hook itself if it has no barb, or the hook will dissolve.

- Never pull on the line of a fish that has swallowed bait. The bait will be in its stomach, and a tug can injure the fish or kill it.
- Release a fish by holding it upright in the water, facing into the current. If there is no current, try "swimming" the fish around until it swims off on its own.

KEEP LEARNING

An important part of fishing is asking questions. An experienced angler knows a lot. If you want to know where to fish or what to use as bait, ask someone. Most people who sell bait or tackle know the local waters. They have fished them and can tell you where to look and what is the best bait to use. But remember . . . anglers won't give away all their secrets. There are some things that you will have to find out on your own. And that's what fishing is all about.

A good angler knows where to find a quiet fishing spot.

Safety Tips

- Don't stand too close to the water's edge.
- Be very cautious if you are fishing from a slippery or steep bank. Don't wade into the water unless you are prepared.
- Never wade into fast-moving water. It can knock you down and pull you under.
- Rocks and logs can be slippery. Wear shoes that have traction, such as cleats.
- Never cast and wade at the same time. Give all your attention to wading.
- Plan ahead before you step. Step slowly, one foot at a time. Never jump from rock to rock.
- If you are going into deeper waters, you must wear rubber waders (boots or overalls).
- If water gets into waders, they will become very heavy and hard to lift in strong currents. Leave the water at once. You're in danger of drowning if a strong current sweeps you downriver.
- Watch out for other people. You want to hook a fish, not a swimmer. Always look behind you before you cast.

- Be aware of the tide at all times.
- Never fish alone when it is dark outside.
- Jetties and piers can be slippery. It is a long fall, and the tide can be very strong around the pillars. Be sure that your shoes have traction.
- Even if you are a good swimmer, wear a life jacket. Strong currents and cold water can be deadly to the best swimmers in the world.
- Always cast straight out over the side of a boat to avoid hooking someone in your boat.
- Many types of fish are dangerous to handle or can be poisonous. They can bite your fingers (bluefish), cut your hands (catfish), or have poisonous tails (stingrays). After catching these types of fish, immediately place them in a water-filled container. Do not try to remove the hook. Cut the line as close as you can to their mouths without putting yourself in danger.

New Words

angler a person who fishes

backcasting a type of casting used by fly fishers

bait a natural food, such as worms or bread, that you use to make the fish bite

bait fishing a common type of freshwater fishing

barb the sharp point at the end of a hook

big-game fishing a type of saltwater fishing that involves going after large ocean fish

bobber a lightweight object, made of wood or plastic, that snaps onto a fishing line

cast to throw your fishing line into the water

catch and release a type of fishing in which the fish are caught and then let go

drag tension in the line

fishing season the time of the year during which you are allowed to fish

fly-fishing freshwater fishing that uses fake flies as bait

freshwater water without salt, such as a river

hook a bent or curved piece of metal used to hook the mouth of a fish

jetties walls that are built out into the water to protect the shore from tides and currents

jig lure that is made with feathers or plastic "hair"

larva a wingless baby fly

leader connects the hook to a fishing line

line the string that you use to bring in the fish

line guide a metal ring that guides the fishing line on a rod

lure man-made object that looks like bait

plug lure that looks like a small fish

reel winds the line in and keeps it from getting tangled

rigging putting together a fishing line using a hook, split shot, and bobber

rod a fishing pole

saltwater water with salt, such as an ocean

sinker a small weight

spinner shiny lure that looks like a small fish

spool holds fishing line

spoon shiny lure that looks like a small fish

tackle fishing equipment

trolling a type of fishing in which a baited line is pulled through the water by a boat

waders tall rubber boots or overalls for wading

For Further Reading

Books
Kugach, Gene. *Freshwater Fishing Tips and Techniques.* Mechanicsburg, PA: Stackpole Books, 1997.

Paulsen, Gary and Ruth Wright Paulsen. *Father Water, Mother Woods: Essays on Fishing and Hunting in the North Woods.* New York: Delacorte Press, 1994.

Smith, Timothy R. *Buck Wilder's Small Fry Fishing Guide: A Complete Introduction to the World of Fishing for Small Fry of All Ages*, Buck Wilder Adventures Series. Williamsburg, MI: Alexander & Smith Publishing, 1995.

Swinney, Geoff and Kate Charlesworth. *Fish Facts.* Gretna, LA: Pelican Publishing Company, Inc., 1994.

Toth, Mike. *The Complete Idiot's Guide to Fishing Basics*, Complete Idiot's Guide. New York: MacMillan Distribution, 1997.

Magazine
American Angler
P.O. Box 434
Mt. Morris, IL 61054

Resources

Fishing Broadcast Network

www.fbnonline.com

This site has it all: articles, product reviews, regional fishing reports, chat room, and interactive games for the freshwater and saltwater angler.

The Fishing Network

www.the-fishing-network.com

If you want news, travel information, weather reports, gear reviews, and other information of use to anglers, this is the spot.

Sporting Adventures

www.spav.com/default.html

This site is full of information about fishing and hunting. It contains links to regional information, including state hunting and fishing departments. It also has tips for good fishing, a photo library, message boards, classifieds, field guides, and much more.

Index

ABOUT THE AUTHOR
Ron Fitzgerald is a freelance writer living in New York City.